IT'S TIME TO LEARN ABOUT COPPERHEAD SNAKES

It's Time to Learn about Copperhead Snakes

Walter the Educator

Silent King Books
A WhichHead Entertainment Imprint

Copyright © 2025 by Walter the Educator

All rights reserved. No part of this book may be reproduced in any manner whatsoever without written per- mission except in the case of brief quotations embodied in critical articles and reviews.

First Printing, 2024

Disclaimer

This book is a literary work; the story is not about specific persons, locations, situations, and/or circumstances unless mentioned in a historical context. Any resemblance to real persons, locations, situations, and/or circumstances is coincidental. This book is for entertainment and informational purposes only. The author and publisher offer this information without warranties expressed or implied. No matter the grounds, neither the author nor the publisher will be accountable for any losses, injuries, or other damages caused by the reader's use of this book. The use of this book acknowledges an understanding and acceptance of this disclaimer.

It's Time to Learn about Copperhead Snakes is a collectible early learning book by Walter the Educator suitable for all ages belonging to Walter the Educator's Time to Eat Book Series. Collect more books at WaltertheEducator.com

USE THE EXTRA SPACE TO TAKE NOTES AND DOCUMENT YOUR MEMORIES

COPPERHEAD SNAKES

The Copperhead is sly and still,

It's Time to Learn about Copperhead Snakes

It hunts by waiting, what a skill!

In leaves of brown and autumn red,

It hides so well, just like it's dead.

Its colors swirl in zigzag bands,

Like ribbons drawn with careful hands.

From copper head to rusty tail,

It blends right in, almost like a veil.

It doesn't grow too very long,

Three feet is right, not big or strong.

But still, this snake you shouldn't tease,

It bites when scared, so give it ease.

It has a head that's shaped like hearts,

With slitted eyes like spooky arts.

It's not a snake that wants to chase,

But give it room, respect its space.

It's Time to Learn about Copperhead Snakes

Copperheads hunt at early night,

When skies grow dim and lose their light.

They sniff the air and sense the heat

Of tiny prey with legs and feet.

They flick their tongues to "taste" the trail

Of hopping mouse or skittering snail.

Then wait and strike with sudden might,

A perfect ambush, not a fight.

Though venom lives inside their bite,

It's not too strong, and not for spite.

They only bite to stay alive,

So step away and let them thrive.

In forests, rocks, and garden beds,

They curl up close like sleepy threads.

So always watch where you may tread,

It's Time to Learn about
Copperhead Snakes

They might be hiding just ahead!

They shed their skin and grow anew,

Their patterns bold, their colors true.

And when the time for babies nears,

They birth them live, no eggs appears!

So now you know this forest snake,

Who hides and hunts for safety's sake.

The Copperhead, though feared by some,

It's Time to Learn about Copperhead Snakes

Just wants to live where it is from.

ABOUT THE CREATOR

Walter the Educator is one of the pseudonyms for Walter Anderson. Formally educated in Chemistry, Business, and Education, he is an educator, an author, a diverse entrepreneur, and he is the son of a disabled war veteran. "Walter the Educator" shares his time between educating and creating. He holds interests and owns several creative projects that entertain, enlighten, enhance, and educate, hoping to inspire and motivate you. Follow, find new works, and stay up to date with Walter the Educator™ at WaltertheEducator.com

www.ingramcontent.com/pod-product-compliance
Lightning Source LLC
LaVergne TN
LVHW051920060526
838201LV00060B/4096